Daily Fitness Log

This booklet contains the following elements to help you plan and monitor your fitness program:

- Program plans
- Weight training logs
- Overall fitness program logs

Mayfield Publishing Company
Mountain View, California
London • Toronto

International Standard Book Number 0-7674-0742-3

Manufactured in the United States of America

10   9   8   7   6   5   4   3

Mayfield Publishing Company
1280 Villa Street
Mountain View, California 94041
(650) 960-3222

Program Plans

1. *Set goals.*

    General fitness goals:

    1. _____

    2. _____

    3. _____

    4. _____

    5. _____

    Specific fitness goals and rewards for achieving them:

Goal	Target date	Reward
_____	_____	_____
_____	_____	_____
_____	_____	_____
_____	_____	_____
_____	_____	_____
_____	_____	_____
_____	_____	_____
_____	_____	_____

    The final page of this booklet contains a place for you to
    record milestones in your fitness program.

2. *Select activities.* Your program should be based around cardiorespiratory endurance exercise, but it should include activities that will develop all the different components of fitness. For example, your program might include bicycling, weight training, and stretching. Fill in the activities you've chosen for the overall program plan on the next page.

   For weight training and stretching programs, you will need to select specific exercises to strengthen and stretch the different muscles of the body. Turn the page and fill in the exercises you've chosen for the weight training and stretching program plans. For each exercise in your weight training program, select a starting weight and number of repetitions and sets; add these to the "Weight Training Program Plan."

3. *Set a target intensity, duration, and frequency for each activity.* Add these to the program plan on the next page. (Refer to your textbook for instructions on how to determine appropriate intensity, duration, and frequency for each activity you've chosen.)

4. *Begin your program.* Use the logs provided here to monitor your progress. Record your fitness milestones on the final page of this booklet.

Overall Program Plan

Activities	Components (Check ✔)					Intensity*	Duration	Frequency (Check ✔)						
	Cardiorespiratory Endurance	Muscular Strength	Muscular Endurance	Flexibility	Body Composition			Monday	Tuesday	Wednesday	Thursday	Friday	Saturday	Sunday
1.														
2.														
3.														
4.														
5.														
6.														

*You should conduct activities for achieving CRE goals at your target heart rate or RPE value.

Weight Training Program Plan

Exercise	Muscle(s) developed	Weight (lb)	Repetitions	Sets

Stretching Program Plan

Exercise	Area(s) stretched

Weight Training Logs

Exercise/Date									
	Wt								
	Sets								
	Reps								
	Wt								
	Sets								
	Reps								
	Wt								
	Sets								
	Reps								
	Wt								
	Sets								
	Reps								
	Wt								
	Sets								
	Reps								
	Wt								
	Sets								
	Reps								
	Wt								
	Sets								
	Reps								
	Wt								
	Sets								
	Reps								
	Wt								
	Sets								
	Reps								
	Wt								
	Sets								
	Reps								
	Wt								
	Sets								
	Reps								
	Wt								
	Sets								
	Reps								

Wt													
Sets													
Reps													
Wt													
Sets													
Reps													
Wt													
Sets													
Reps													
Wt													
Sets													
Reps													
Wt													
Sets													
Reps													
Wt													
Sets													
Reps													
Wt													
Sets													
Reps													
Wt													
Sets													
Reps													
Wt													
Sets													
Reps													
Wt													
Sets													
Reps													
Wt													
Sets													
Reps													

Exercise/Date									
	Wt								
	Sets								
	Reps								
	Wt								
	Sets								
	Reps								
	Wt								
	Sets								
	Reps								
	Wt								
	Sets								
	Reps								
	Wt								
	Sets								
	Reps								
	Wt								
	Sets								
	Reps								
	Wt								
	Sets								
	Reps								
	Wt								
	Sets								
	Reps								
	Wt								
	Sets								
	Reps								
	Wt								
	Sets								
	Reps								
	Wt								
	Sets								
	Reps								
	Wt								
	Sets								
	Reps								

Wt												
Sets												
Reps												
Wt												
Sets												
Reps												
Wt												
Sets												
Reps												
Wt												
Sets												
Reps												
Wt												
Sets												
Reps												
Wt												
Sets												
Reps												
Wt												
Sets												
Reps												
Wt												
Sets												
Reps												
Wt												
Sets												
Reps												
Wt												
Sets												
Reps												
Wt												
Sets												
Reps												
Wt												
Sets												
Reps												
Wt												
Sets												
Reps												

Exercise/Date								
	Wt							
	Sets							
	Reps							
	Wt							
	Sets							
	Reps							
	Wt							
	Sets							
	Reps							
	Wt							
	Sets							
	Reps							
	Wt							
	Sets							
	Reps							
	Wt							
	Sets							
	Reps							
	Wt							
	Sets							
	Reps							
	Wt							
	Sets							
	Reps							
	Wt							
	Sets							
	Reps							
	Wt							
	Sets							
	Reps							
	Wt							
	Sets							
	Reps							
	Wt							
	Sets							
	Reps							

Wt												
Sets												
Reps												
Wt												
Sets												
Reps												
Wt												
Sets												
Reps												
Wt												
Sets												
Reps												
Wt												
Sets												
Reps												
Wt												
Sets												
Reps												
Wt												
Sets												
Reps												
Wt												
Sets												
Reps												
Wt												
Sets												
Reps												
Wt												
Sets												
Reps												
Wt												
Sets												
Reps												
Wt												
Sets												
Reps												

Exercise/Date									
	Wt								
	Sets								
	Reps								
	Wt								
	Sets								
	Reps								
	Wt								
	Sets								
	Reps								
	Wt								
	Sets								
	Reps								
	Wt								
	Sets								
	Reps								
	Wt								
	Sets								
	Reps								
	Wt								
	Sets								
	Reps								
	Wt								
	Sets								
	Reps								
	Wt								
	Sets								
	Reps								
	Wt								
	Sets								
	Reps								
	Wt								
	Sets								
	Reps								
	Wt								
	Sets								
	Reps								
	Wt								
	Sets								
	Reps								

Wt												
Sets												
Reps												
Wt												
Sets												
Reps												
Wt												
Sets												
Reps												
Wt												
Sets												
Reps												
Wt												
Sets												
Reps												
Wt												
Sets												
Reps												
Wt												
Sets												
Reps												
Wt												
Sets												
Reps												
Wt												
Sets												
Reps												
Wt												
Sets												
Reps												
Wt												
Sets												
Reps												

Weight Training Log

Weight Training Log

Exercise/Date									
	Wt								
	Sets								
	Reps								
	Wt								
	Sets								
	Reps								
	Wt								
	Sets								
	Reps								
	Wt								
	Sets								
	Reps								
	Wt								
	Sets								
	Reps								
	Wt								
	Sets								
	Reps								
	Wt								
	Sets								
	Reps								
	Wt								
	Sets								
	Reps								
	Wt								
	Sets								
	Reps								
	Wt								
	Sets								
	Reps								
	Wt								
	Sets								
	Reps								
	Wt								
	Sets								
	Reps								

Wt												
Sets												
Reps												
Wt												
Sets												
Reps												
Wt												
Sets												
Reps												
Wt												
Sets												
Reps												
Wt												
Sets												
Reps												
Wt												
Sets												
Reps												
Wt												
Sets												
Reps												
Wt												
Sets												
Reps												
Wt												
Sets												
Reps												
Wt												
Sets												
Reps												
Wt												
Sets												
Reps												
Wt												
Sets												
Reps												

Exercise/Date									
	Wt								
	Sets								
	Reps								
	Wt								
	Sets								
	Reps								
	Wt								
	Sets								
	Reps								
	Wt								
	Sets								
	Reps								
	Wt								
	Sets								
	Reps								
	Wt								
	Sets								
	Reps								
	Wt								
	Sets								
	Reps								
	Wt								
	Sets								
	Reps								
	Wt								
	Sets								
	Reps								
	Wt								
	Sets								
	Reps								
	Wt								
	Sets								
	Reps								
	Wt								
	Sets								
	Reps								
	Wt								
	Sets								
	Reps								

Wt												
Sets													
Reps													
Wt													
Sets													
Reps													
Wt													
Sets													
Reps													
Wt													
Sets													
Reps													
Wt													
Sets													
Reps													
Wt													
Sets													
Reps													
Wt													
Sets													
Reps													
Wt													
Sets													
Reps													
Wt													
Sets													
Reps													
Wt													
Sets													
Reps													
Wt													
Sets													
Reps													

Weight Training Log

Exercise/Date									
	Wt								
	Sets								
	Reps								
	Wt								
	Sets								
	Reps								
	Wt								
	Sets								
	Reps								
	Wt								
	Sets								
	Reps								
	Wt								
	Sets								
	Reps								
	Wt								
	Sets								
	Reps								
	Wt								
	Sets								
	Reps								
	Wt								
	Sets								
	Reps								
	Wt								
	Sets								
	Reps								
	Wt								
	Sets								
	Reps								
	Wt								
	Sets								
	Reps								
	Wt								
	Sets								
	Reps								

Wt											
Sets											
Reps											
Wt											
Sets											
Reps											
Wt											
Sets											
Reps											
Wt											
Sets											
Reps											
Wt											
Sets											
Reps											
Wt											
Sets											
Reps											
Wt											
Sets											
Reps											
Wt											
Sets											
Reps											
Wt											
Sets											
Reps											
Wt											
Sets											
Reps											
Wt											
Sets											
Reps											
Wt											
Sets											
Reps											

Weight Training Log

Exercise/Date								
	Wt							
	Sets							
	Reps							
	Wt							
	Sets							
	Reps							
	Wt							
	Sets							
	Reps							
	Wt							
	Sets							
	Reps							
	Wt							
	Sets							
	Reps							
	Wt							
	Sets							
	Reps							
	Wt							
	Sets							
	Reps							
	Wt							
	Sets							
	Reps							
	Wt							
	Sets							
	Reps							
	Wt							
	Sets							
	Reps							
	Wt							
	Sets							
	Reps							
	Wt							
	Sets							
	Reps							

Wt											
Sets											
Reps											
Wt											
Sets											
Reps											
Wt											
Sets											
Reps											
Wt											
Sets											
Reps											
Wt											
Sets											
Reps											
Wt											
Sets											
Reps											
Wt											
Sets											
Reps											
Wt											
Sets											
Reps											
Wt											
Sets											
Reps											
Wt											
Sets											
Reps											
Wt											
Sets											
Reps											
Wt											
Sets											
Reps											

Weight Training Log

Exercise/Date									
	Wt								
	Sets								
	Reps								
	Wt								
	Sets								
	Reps								
	Wt								
	Sets								
	Reps								
	Wt								
	Sets								
	Reps								
	Wt								
	Sets								
	Reps								
	Wt								
	Sets								
	Reps								
	Wt								
	Sets								
	Reps								
	Wt								
	Sets								
	Reps								
	Wt								
	Sets								
	Reps								
	Wt								
	Sets								
	Reps								
	Wt								
	Sets								
	Reps								
	Wt								
	Sets								
	Reps								
	Wt								
	Sets								
	Reps								

Wt												
Sets												
Reps												
Wt												
Sets												
Reps												
Wt												
Sets												
Reps												
Wt												
Sets												
Reps												
Wt												
Sets												
Reps												
Wt												
Sets												
Reps												
Wt												
Sets												
Reps												
Wt												
Sets												
Reps												
Wt												
Sets												
Reps												
Wt												
Sets												
Reps												
Wt												
Sets												
Reps												
Wt												
Sets												
Reps												

Weight Training Log

Exercise/Date								
	Wt							
	Sets							
	Reps							
	Wt							
	Sets							
	Reps							
	Wt							
	Sets							
	Reps							
	Wt							
	Sets							
	Reps							
	Wt							
	Sets							
	Reps							
	Wt							
	Sets							
	Reps							
	Wt							
	Sets							
	Reps							
	Wt							
	Sets							
	Reps							
	Wt							
	Sets							
	Reps							
	Wt							
	Sets							
	Reps							
	Wt							
	Sets							
	Reps							
	Wt							
	Sets							
	Reps							

Wt												
Sets												
Reps												
Wt												
Sets												
Reps												
Wt												
Sets												
Reps												
Wt												
Sets												
Reps												
Wt												
Sets												
Reps												
Wt												
Sets												
Reps												
Wt												
Sets												
Reps												
Wt												
Sets												
Reps												
Wt												
Sets												
Reps												
Wt												
Sets												
Reps												
Wt												
Sets												
Reps												
Wt												
Sets												
Reps												

Overall Fitness Program Logs

To use the overall fitness program logs, fill in the activities that are part of your program. Each day, note the distance and/or time you complete for each activity. For flexibility or weight training workouts, you may prefer just to enter a check mark each time you complete a workout. At the end of each week, total your distances and/or times.

Date _____

Activity	M	Tu	W	Th	F	Sa	Su	Weekly Total
1.								
2.								
3.								
4.								
5.								
6.								

Date _____

Activity	M	Tu	W	Th	F	Sa	Su	Weekly Total
1.								
2.								
3.								
4.								
5.								
6.								

Date _____

Activity	M	Tu	W	Th	F	Sa	Su	Weekly Total
1.								
2.								
3.								
4.								
5.								
6.								

Fitness Program Log

Date _____

Activity	M	Tu	W	Th	F	Sa	Su	Weekly Total
1.								
2.								
3.								
4.								
5.								
6.								

Date _____

Activity	M	Tu	W	Th	F	Sa	Su	Weekly Total
1.								
2.								
3.								
4.								
5.								
6.								

Date _____

Activity	M	Tu	W	Th	F	Sa	Su	Weekly Total
1.								
2.								
3.								
4.								
5.								
6.								

Date _____

Activity	M	Tu	W	Th	F	Sa	Su	Weekly Total
1.								
2.								
3.								
4.								
5.								
6.								

Date _____

	Activity	M	Tu	W	Th	F	Sa	Su	Weekly Total
1.									
2.									
3.									
4.									
5.									
6.									

Date _____

	Activity	M	Tu	W	Th	F	Sa	Su	Weekly Total
1.									
2.									
3.									
4.									
5.									
6.									

Date _____

Activity	M	Tu	W	Th	F	Sa	Su	Weekly Total
1.								
2.								
3.								
4.								
5.								
6.								

Date _____

Activity	M	Tu	W	Th	F	Sa	Su	Weekly Total
1.								
2.								
3.								
4.								
5.								
6.								

Date _____

Activity	M	Tu	W	Th	F	Sa	Su	Weekly Total
1.								
2.								
3.								
4.								
5.								
6.								

Date _____

Activity	M	Tu	W	Th	F	Sa	Su	Weekly Total
1.								
2.								
3.								
4.								
5.								
6.								

Date _____

Activity	M	Tu	W	Th	F	Sa	Su	Weekly Total
1.								
2.								
3.								
4.								
5.								
6.								

Date _____

Activity	M	Tu	W	Th	F	Sa	Su	Weekly Total
1.								
2.								
3.								
4.								
5.								
6.								

Date _____

Activity	M	Tu	W	Th	F	Sa	Su	Weekly Total
1.								
2.								
3.								
4.								
5.								
6.								

Date _____

Activity	M	Tu	W	Th	F	Sa	Su	Weekly Total
1.								
2.								
3.								
4.								
5.								
6.								

Date _____

Activity	M	Tu	W	Th	F	Sa	Su	Weekly Total
1.								
2.								
3.								
4.								
5.								
6.								

Date _____

Activity	M	Tu	W	Th	F	Sa	Su	Weekly Total
1.								
2.								
3.								
4.								
5.								
6.								

Fitness Program Log

Date _____

Activity	M	Tu	W	Th	F	Sa	Su	Weekly Total
1.								
2.								
3.								
4.								
5.								
6.								

Date _____

Activity	M	Tu	W	Th	F	Sa	Su	Weekly Total
1.								
2.								
3.								
4.								
5.								
6.								

Date _____

Activity	M	Tu	W	Th	F	Sa	Su	Weekly Total
1.								
2.								
3.								
4.								
5.								
6.								

Date _____

Activity	M	Tu	W	Th	F	Sa	Su	Weekly Total
1.								
2.								
3.								
4.								
5.								
6.								

Date _____

Activity	M	Tu	W	Th	F	Sa	Su	Weekly Total
1.								
2.								
3.								
4.								
5.								
6.								

Date _____

Activity	M	Tu	W	Th	F	Sa	Su	Weekly Total
1.								
2.								
3.								
4.								
5.								
6.								

Date _____

Activity	M	Tu	W	Th	F	Sa	Su	Weekly Total
1.								
2.								
3.								
4.								
5.								
6.								

Date _____

Activity	M	Tu	W	Th	F	Sa	Su	Weekly Total
1.								
2.								
3.								
4.								
5.								
6.								

Date _____

Activity	M	Tu	W	Th	F	Sa	Su	Weekly Total
1.								
2.								
3.								
4.								
5.								
6.								

Date _____

Activity	M	Tu	W	Th	F	Sa	Su	Weekly Total
1.								
2.								
3.								
4.								
5.								
6.								

Date _____

Activity	M	Tu	W	Th	F	Sa	Su	Weekly Total
1.								
2.								
3.								
4.								
5.								
6.								

Date _____

Activity	M	Tu	W	Th	F	Sa	Su	Weekly Total
1.								
2.								
3.								
4.								
5.								
6.								

Date _____

Activity	M	Tu	W	Th	F	Sa	Su	Weekly Total
1.								
2.								
3.								
4.								
5.								
6.								

Date _____

Activity	M	Tu	W	Th	F	Sa	Su	Weekly Total
1.								
2.								
3.								
4.								
5.								
6.								

Date _____

Activity	M	Tu	W	Th	F	Sa	Su	Weekly Total
1.								
2.								
3.								
4.								
5.								
6.								

Date _____

Activity	M	Tu	W	Th	F	Sa	Su	Weekly Total
1.								
2.								
3.								
4.								
5.								
6.								

Fitness Program Log

Date _____

Activity	M	Tu	W	Th	F	Sa	Su	Weekly Total
1.								
2.								
3.								
4.								
5.								
6.								

Date _____

Activity	M	Tu	W	Th	F	Sa	Su	Weekly Total
1.								
2.								
3.								
4.								
5.								
6.								

Date _____

Activity	M	Tu	W	Th	F	Sa	Su	Weekly Total
1.								
2.								
3.								
4.								
5.								
6.								

Date _____

Activity	M	Tu	W	Th	F	Sa	Su	Weekly Total
1.								
2.								
3.								
4.								
5.								
6.								

Fitness Program Milestones

Milestone	Date	Reward